Set Apart

a poetry collection about the Christian journey from worldly to godly

Angelique McVey

ISBN: 979-8-218-16624-3

Once you were alienated from God and were enemies in your minds because of your evil behavior. But now he has reconciled you by Christ's physical body through death to present you holy in his sight, without blemish and free from accusation.

Colossians 1:21-22

CONTENTS

To my readers,

The gospel is only good news to those who first
understand the bad news. This is my heart behind
the structure of this poetry collection. If you find
yourself feeling discouraged as you read the first
section, that is the point! Keep reading to be
immersed in the good news of the gospel.

I share these poems humbly, knowing that I am
continually learning how to balance grace and truth
on these complex topics. The poems in this book
are based on my personal convictions and current
interpretation of Scripture, and they are not meant
to be an exact description of every Christian's
journey.

My hope is that this collection gives you a glimpse
of God's incredible redemption story. I pray that
my words can uplift and edify you, but only God's
Word can truly transform you. Please open the
Bible and read it for yourself to learn more about
the saving work of Jesus Christ, a free gift available
to all who trust in Him and surrender their lives to
Him.

Sincerely,

Angelique McVey

Depraved

the condition of humanity before Jesus; to be enslaved to our sinful, wicked, and self-seeking nature

As for you, you were dead in your transgressions and sins, in which you used to live when you followed the ways of this world and of the ruler of the kingdom of the air, the spirit who is now at work in those who are disobedient. All of us also lived among them at one time, gratifying the cravings of our flesh and following its desires and thoughts. Like the rest, we were by nature deserving of wrath.

Ephesians 2:1-3

Tainted

This body of flesh

breaks its own bones

and scars its own skin.

This body of flesh

curses its Maker

and coddles its sin.

This body of flesh

is an enemy of God

and a lover of self.

This body of flesh,

left to itself, would

willingly walk into hell.

The pursuit of death

The voices of culture

partner with the prince of darkness

and whisper words of worldly wisdom

to a people desiring to feel alive.

"Find peace with yourself

by embracing your sins

and chasing your desires.

You're perfectly made,

so pursue what you please

even if it kills you inside."

There is a way that appears to be right, but in the end it leads to death.

Proverbs 14:12

Before Jesus

I was formless and empty.

Just as the world was

before the Creator

spoke light into darkness,

so I was before the Light

awakened my darkened heart.

I was weary and enslaved.

Just as Israel was

before her Deliverer

led her to peace,

so I was before the Redeemer

set me free to set me apart.

Foolish

You asked for my heart,

and I guarded it with my life.

For I delighted in my darkness

though I claimed to love the light.

I walked through the motions,

but my heart was far from You.

For my flesh was my true master;

it controlled my every move.

You asked for my heart,

and I refused to give it up.

For though I claimed to know You,

my flesh was my true love.

For although they knew God, they neither glorified him as God nor gave thanks to him, but their thinking became futile and their foolish hearts were darkened.

Romans 1:21

Pretend

The idol of self is the hardest to tear down.

The crown is nearly impossible to surrender.

For I have consistently chosen

to place my heart on the throne,

pretending the King doesn't really exist

so I could continue my pretend reign.

*In his pride the wicked man does not seek him; in
all his thoughts there is no room for God.*

Psalm 10:4

Forbidden fruit

"Did God really say that was sin?"
the serpent asked,
just as he did in Eden.

I knew God's command,
yet I still chose
to reach out my hand,

for I had begun to believe
that God was withholding
something good from me.

I rejected Him
because I thought
I'd be happier in my sins,

indulging in sin's sweet taste
then cursing God
for my stomach ache.

Wretched

Wretched man that I am.

I looked into the eyes of my Savior

as He suffered on the cross,

and I chose my sins instead.

As He died for me,

I told Him I'd rather live for myself.

*This is the verdict: Light has come into the world,
but people loved darkness instead of light because
their deeds were evil.*

John 3:19

Empty vessel

I live in a land that seeks healing

in the absence of a Healer.

I see others looking for light within

rather than looking above.

I followed the world's advice

and labored to heal my heart with self-love.

But I was still broken.

None of my efforts were enough.

No matter how much love I gifted myself,

I never truly felt loved.

In the absence of the Beloved,

I was just an empty vessel trying to fill myself up.

Corpses

The god of the world

sells us luxury, sex, and beauty.

He erects billboards and hires celebrities

to persuade us we're only valuable if we're pretty.

So we spend our paychecks

trying to look like princesses,

but we're just corpses playing dress-up.

We're convinced we'll feel alive

when our wallets are thicker

and our lips are fuller,

but our greed and vanity are strangling us.

We keep searching for life

on the path of death.

*For everything in the world—the lust of the flesh,
the lust of the eyes, and the pride of life—comes
not from the Father but from the world.*

1 John 2:16

Chains

I see a world

where pleasure is priority.

Its slaves are lusting for luxury,

on a greedy quest for gratification

that never seems to please,

chasing after the wind

for just a taste of a breeze.

I see a world

where souls are squandered.

The slaves dress themselves in rotting rags

and indulge in anything they see,

searching for freedom

by trying on different chains.

No wonder they long to be free.

*At one time we too were foolish, disobedient,
deceived and enslaved by all kinds of passions and
pleasures.*

Titus 3:3a

Vice of vanity

I dressed to attract the world,

and I colored my lips with pride.

I harbored haughtiness in my heart

and sought attention in each stride.

Soaking up self-love

but drowning in depravity,

I volunteered my every move

to the vicious vice of vanity.

Babylon

The national anthem of Babylon:

Do what you want.

There is no royal law in this city,

for each man's king is his own heart.

The pawns of satan play games and

corrupt the minds of the youth.

Children are taught morality is relative,

that there is no such thing as truth.

Indeed, the national anthem rings true

for everyone does whatever they please.

And the city grows in corruption,

becoming a haven for all that's unclean.

Lusting for love

Purity is a curse word today.

Society teaches our children

to pursue their pleasures

as long as they do it safely.

But no amount of protection

can prevent a broken heart.

So, our children grow up

moving from bed to bed,

seeking more intimacy

but feeling less and less.

They keep crawling back under the sheets,

trying to create love out of lust,

trying to feel something other than numb.

The broad road

Wide is the road of no morals.

Street signs are no more.

Lawlessness is worshiped.

Selfish ambition is adored.

Right and wrong are offensive.

Feelings are the guide.

The truth is ever-changing.

You can drive on either side.

Wide is the road of no morals,

and vast is the destruction it brings.

For this is the fate of a world

where everyone drives however they please.

Polluted

With the taste of the forbidden fruit

still on our lips,

we curse God for our pain.

Yet, the blood is on our hands

for we polluted this land.

We are the ones to blame.

*Therefore, just as sin entered the world through
one man, and death through sin, and in this way
death came to all people, because all sinned.*

Romans 5:12

Rainbow

As in the days of Noah,

the wicked laugh at the coming judgment

and spit in the face of their Judge.

Yet God sits on His throne

watching His rainbow fill the sky,

and He withholds a little longer.

He looked down on you

when your heart was cold toward Him

and sin consumed your life,

and He longed for you to come to Him.

He looked to His rainbow in the sky,

and He withheld a little longer.

*The Lord is not slow in keeping his promise, as
some understand slowness. Instead he is
patient with you, not wanting anyone to perish, but
everyone to come to repentance.*

2 Peter 3:9

Miracle

The depravity of the world dwells within us all.

We all have reached for the fatal fruit,
persuaded by the father of lies.
And like the Tower of Babel,
we've built our egos to the sky.

But we were created to be different
and called to be set apart.
The Creator of Souls is knocking,
desiring to dwell within each heart.

He wants to strip you of your pride
and transform your lofty view.
The Miracle Worker Himself
wants to work a miracle in you.

The great exchange

Why do you keep going back

to the sins that

weigh you down?

Your King is waiting

to exchange your chains

for a crown.

Rescued

You've been trying to climb out

of the darkness yourself,

but your grave has only grown deeper.

His love is deeper still.

You cannot rescue yourself,

but Someone has already

reached down to rescue you.

If only you'd reach up and grab His hand.

*He has rescued us from the dominion of
darkness and brought us into the kingdom of the
Son he loves, in whom we have redemption, the
forgiveness of sins.*

Colossians 1:13-14

Reconciled

the restorative work of the atoning death
and resurrection of Jesus; to be befriended
by God while we were still enemies

*God demonstrates his own love for us in this:
While we were still sinners, Christ died for us.
Since we have now been justified by his
blood, how much more shall we be saved from
God's wrath through him! For if, while we were
God's enemies, we were reconciled to him
through the death of his Son, how much more,
having been reconciled, shall we be saved through
his life!*

Romans 5:8-10

Cancelled debts

All the gold buried beneath the earth

could not pay the debts I owed.

I saw no hope in my hands, no worth in my works.

My efforts only proved to dig a deeper hole,

so I accepted my fate as a slave to my shame,

rejecting the well where the living water flows.

But in my bondage, Christ called me by name,

ransoming me from the burdens I owed,

bearing God's wrath though I was to blame.

For the first time in my life, I understood hope.

Though I was unworthy, He clothed me in worth.

Though I was a slave, He made me His own.

*So you are no longer a slave, but God's child; and
since you are his child, God has made you also an
heir.*

Galatians 4:7

Different gardens

In the garden of Eden,

God's perfect creation

selfishly chose to bring death into

a perfect world of love.

In the garden of Gethsemane,

God's perfect Son

lovingly chose to bring life into

a selfish world of sin.

Advocate

Christ pleaded with the Father

to have mercy on Him

as blood dripped from His pores:

His humanity on full display.

Our sins struck His skin over and over.

Our iniquities asphyxiated His lungs.

Still, He cried out for our forgiveness.

Now, He pleads with the Father

to have mercy on us,

pointing to the eternal scars He bore:

His love has made a way.

If anybody does sin, we have an advocate with the Father—Jesus Christ, the Righteous One.

1 John 2:1b

What a Savior

Jesus emptied Himself

of every heavenly comfort

while we were still worshiping

the comforts of the world.

He gave up power and glory

to serve the very ones who betrayed Him.

He willingly extended His arms to death,

looking forward to an eternity

of embracing the very sinners

who nailed Him to the cross.

He reached toward us with bleeding hands

while our hands were still bleeding

from the tight grip we had on our sins.

What a Savior, to sacrifice Himself for us

before we even knew we needed saved.

Gospel

Righteous and just,

yet gracious and kind.

His character never contradicts:

He hates and loves at the same time.

He is perfectly holy;

we are wretchedly wicked.

Though all evidence condemns us,

here we are: standing acquitted.

For He loved us enough to sacrifice

the perfect and spotless Lamb.

Each nail in His hand tore the veil between

sinful man and the Great I Am.

We deserved a criminal's death,

but Christ carried the cross in our place.

God justly judged sin in Christ's sinless flesh

so He could justify us by His grace.

*God presented Christ as a sacrifice of atonement
… to demonstrate his righteousness at the present
time, so as to be just and the one who justifies
those who have faith in Jesus.*

Romans 3:25-26

King

All was dim and dreary

on the night they

killed my Lord.

But the darkened tomb

could not subdue

the One who lights the world.

The cries of sorrow

swiftly changed

to songs of victory.

For my Lord died

like a criminal,

but He rose a Mighty King.

Priests

God's power was made known

as the sky grew dark.

The veil was torn,

and He turned sinners into priests.

God's glory was shown

as light pierced the gloom.

The stone was rolled away,

and He turned corpses into kings.

*[He] has made us to be a kingdom and priests to
serve his God and Father—to him be glory and
power for ever and ever! Amen.*

Revelation 1:6

Love wins

Jesus won my hardened heart.

He stepped down from glory

to walk these muddy waters with me.

As stones were throne my way,

He stepped in front of them

and endured what I deserved.

As He thirsted on the cross,

He offered me living water—

the kind that cleanses through and through.

He saw my hardened heart,

and He softened it

with His final breath.

He won my hardened heart,

not with force

but with sacrificial love.

This is how we know what love is: Jesus Christ laid down his life for us.

1 John 3:16

Clean

My Judge and my Attorney—

how could this be?

You know the punishment I deserve

but find a way to set me free.

My Father and my Savior—

how great is Your love for me!

You remove me from the mud,

and You wash Your child clean.

Saved

The Holy of Holies must punish

a sinner as wretched as me.

For I cannot enter into His sanctuary

with a heart that is this unclean.

But God saved me from Himself

by pouring out His wrath on Christ:

my sinless Savior suffering

as a substitutionary sacrifice.

Now, the Holy of Holies is pleased

with a sinner as wretched as me.

He enters into my heart to begin

cleansing and washing me.

For God saved me for Himself,

promising to make me more like Christ:

my sinless Savior resurrected

so I can walk in His glorious light.

*He himself bore our sins in his body on the cross,
so that we might die to sins and live for
righteousness; by his wounds you have been
healed.*

1 Peter 2:24

Healer

My God who touched the lepers

touches my heart,

cleansing it of all that is unclean.

My God who commanded the lame to walk

directs my every step,

making straight my wandering feet.

My God who restored sight to the blind

rescues me from darkness,

giving me eyes that truly see.

My God who fashioned miracles

offers me the greatest one of all:

His perfect life laid down for me.

Atonement

The Man of Sorrows

offers me joy.

The Light of the World

carries my darkness.

The Good Shepherd

walks to the slaughter.

His chastisement

clears my every record of wrong.

His beaten body

heals my every wound.

His agonizing cries

produce psalms of praise in me.

The Almighty God

emptied Himself to fill me up.

Maybe one day I'll finally grasp

such a perfect love.

He was pierced for our transgressions, he was crushed for our iniquities; the punishment that brought us peace was on him, and by his wounds we are healed.

Isaiah 53:5

Barabbas

He clothed Himself with chains,

and they set Barabbas free.

He stained His skin with stripes,

and they declared Barabbas clean.

He was executed like a criminal

though Barabbas committed the crime.

He willingly walked to death,

and Barabbas was given new life.

Barabbas deserved what Jesus endured,

and now, I finally see

Jesus took my place that day,

and Barabbas is actually me.

Mercy

Reconciled: to be brought home.

I've chosen to walk this world alone,

estranged from my Perfect Father;

I deserve to be disowned.

The veil separates me from His holy throne,

yet He tears the veil to befriend me

and reconcile me as His own.

Justified: to be made right.

I'm standing in the courthouse of the skies

with the Holy Judge before me;

there's fire in His eyes.

The evidence against me is piled high,

yet His mercy clears my record,

and He declares me justified.

Forsaken

Wrath, poured upon Him

like a raging storm

so I can be submerged

in His saving sea.

He felt forsaken

as He poured out His life

so I can be assured

He will never forsake me.

God has said, "Never will I leave you; never will I forsake you."

Hebrews 13:5b

Among the mockers

I heard my voice among the mockers.

I found my face within the crowd.

"Crucify Him!" we shouted,

yet He did not make a sound.

I saw my sins within the lash marks,

my selfish wrongs in every slit.

And as my Savior wailed in pain,

my hands controlled the whip.

I followed Him to Calvary,

to the place He was defamed.

I heard my scoffs among the soldiers,

and on each nail, I read my name.

Then I saw myself in the thief on the cross,

beside Him as He died.

"Forgive me, Lord," I begged Him,

and for the debts I owed, I cried.

He looked at me, losing breath:

broken, beaten, and bruised.

And the perfect Lord forgave me,

"Daughter, I did this all for you."

Abba

Oh, how sweet is my God!

How loving is my Abba Father,

that He calls me out of slavery

and renames me His precious daughter.

Oh, how deep is our bond!

How close is my God to me,

that He looks on me with love

and leaves His wrath at Calvary.

Gift

The God of Ages

bore the guilt of mankind

to offer the guilty

the free gift of life.

He hands me this gift.

I hand Him my soul.

I give Him every piece of me.

In return, He makes me whole.

For it is by grace you have been saved, through faith—and this is not from yourselves, it is the gift of God— not by works, so that no one can boast.

Ephesians 2:8-9

Restoring Eden

He breathes restoration
into barren ground:

sprouting flowers in my cracking clay
and bringing life to my desert of shame.

In my impoverished state,
living water pours down:

sprinkling the earth with His cleansing flow
and ushering in His kingdom of hope.

He has made whole
my once infertile soul:

tilling my heart to prepare me for His plan
and restoring Eden in my once desolate land.

No trace

He hangs a millstone around my sins

and tosses them into the sea:

never to be recovered again,

never to be traced back to me.

*You will tread our sins underfoot and hurl all our
iniquities into the depths of the sea.*

Micah 7:19b

Redemption

What does it mean to be redeemed?

Reconciled by His love:

Christ's righteousness covers me.

Ransomed by His blood:

I have been set free.

Risen from the grave:

His resurrection awakens me.

Repurchased as His child:

the safest place to be.

Found

My wandering heart was far away,

yet my Good Shepherd sought me.

I was feral and without a home,

yet with His blood, He bought me.

He guided me to greener pastures

and cleansed my wounds from thorny ground.

He treated me like a royal heir,

His precious treasure He had found.

*You are a chosen people, a royal priesthood, a
holy nation, God's special possession, that you
may declare the praises of him who called you out
of darkness into his wonderful light.*

1 Peter 2:9

Victory

We don't live in the days before the empty tomb:

the days of waiting,

the days of fear,

the days of uncertainty.

We live in the days where Christ is living:

the days of renewing,

the days of confidence,

the days of peace.

For His resurrection proved His promises

and verified His victory.

When Christ's buried body breathed again,

He breathed new life in me.

Jesus said to her, "I am the resurrection and the life. The one who believes in me will live, even though they die."

John 11:25

Selah

There's no other response but worship,

for He is worthy of all my praise.

That I, a wretched sinner,

am loved by the Ancient of Days.

There's no other response but thanksgiving,

for He is worthy of all my love.

That I, a lawbreaking criminal,

have a place in His kingdom above.

Humbled

the awareness of our own sinfulness and the realization of how much we need Jesus; to be brought low in the presence of God's glory and grace

To some who were confident of their own righteousness and looked down on everyone else, Jesus told this parable: "Two men went up to the temple to pray, one a Pharisee and the other a tax collector. The Pharisee stood by himself and prayed: 'God, I thank you that I am not like other people—robbers, evildoers, adulterers—or even like this tax collector. I fast twice a week and give a tenth of all I get.' But the tax collector stood at a distance. He would not even look up to heaven, but beat his breast and said, 'God, have mercy on me, a sinner.' I tell you that this man, rather than the other, went home justified before God. For all those who exalt themselves will be humbled, and those who humble themselves will be exalted."

Luke 18:9-14

Lifted lamentations

My sins number among the stars in the sky,

yet His mercies are new each morning.

My sins weigh on my chest like bricks of shame,

yet He lifts them and carries them to the cross.

My sins drip from His skin in droplets of blood,

yet He forgives

    and forgives

        and forgives.

Because of the LORD's great love we are not consumed, for his compassions never fail. They are new every morning; great is your faithfulness.

Lamentations 3:22-23

Marvelous

I repent for my lack of repentance.

I've offered You lip service all my life

as if that was enough.

I was not broken by my sin

nor convinced of Your marvelous love.

I was taught of my own sinfulness,

but my eyes had not yet seen.

So I gave You my empty works,

just like those woeful Pharisees.

I was a Christian by name,

but my affections were far from You.

But there came a day

when You broke down my walls

to build my heart anew.

There, I saw the depravity of my sin

and Christ bearing my guilt and shame.

In my humility, You were glorified

as You showed me Your marvelous grace.

Springs of mercy

Lord, cleanse this anxious heart

in living water.

Grow gardens of grace

in the dry cracks of my soul.

My perfectionism has left me wilted.

My striving has dried me of praise.

I have no first fruits to offer as worship,

for my own efforts have yet to produce a yield.

Lord, purify this wandering heart

 in precious blood.

Here I am before You,

repenting of the perfectionism

that I've nurtured in my soul.

I've labored to grow a glorious garden,

and because I placed hope in myself,

my trust in the Vine withered and died.

Lord, accept this contrite heart

as a fragrant sacrifice.

Water my barren land with Your Spirit

so I can dwell in Your pasture of peace:

the promised land of milk and honey.

Lead me again and again to springs of mercy,

reminding me that it's You— only You.

This garden is Yours to till, not mine.

Remain in me, as I also remain in you. No branch can bear fruit by itself; it must remain in the vine. Neither can you bear fruit unless you remain in me.

John 15:4

Burdened

Burdened by my guilt and shame,

I trudge toward His gentle voice

which whispers, "Come to me."

Longing to have this yoke lifted,

craving a quieted soul,

yearning to finally feel free.

Gently, He points me to the cross

where my burdens crushed His lungs:

His body, void of breath, so I could finally breathe.

*Come to me, all you who are weary and burdened,
and I will give you rest. Take my yoke upon you
and learn from me, for I am gentle and humble in
heart, and you will find rest for your souls.*

Matthew 11:28-29

Identity

The world told me:

"You are enough,

you are a good person,

you are worthy,"

yet I felt empty every day.

I was chasing self-love as if

it had the power to make me whole.

I searched for worth in worldly terms,

neglecting the hunger in my soul.

Then God told me:

"You are not enough,

you are not a good person,

you are not worthy,

yet I love you anyway."

What humbling and comforting words,

knowing my worth doesn't depend on me.

My identity is not in the human I am

but in my Loving Lord who died for me.

Washed

You washed Judas' feet,

the same feet that fled to betray You.

On that treacherous night,

Your love for us radiated

through the gloom.

You washed my heart that night,

the same heart that's inclined to wander.

I've betrayed You like Judas.

I've denied You like Peter.

Yet, You washed my feet.

Jesus, I am so undeserving,

yet You still wash me clean.

Undeserved

Judgment is earned;

grace is undeserved.

I've earned judgment

in every lie I've told,

every hateful word I've spoken,

and every immoral thought I've pondered.

But each sin was forgiven

in every strike to His back,

every thorn pressed against His scalp,

and every nail hammered through His flesh.

He received an undeserved judgment

so I could receive undeserved grace.

But because of his great love for us, God, who is rich in mercy, made us alive with Christ even when we were dead in transgressions—it is by grace you have been saved.

Ephesians 2:4-5

Egypt

He saved me from death's grip,

carried me through the wilderness,

and showed me His promised land,

yet I told Him I wanted to return to Egypt.

How foolish I was

to be given abundant life

then run back toward death.

How gracious He was to save me again.

Heart of flesh

I have chosen my flesh again and again,

hid from You to indulge in my sin.

I'm just as guilty as

the evil on death row.

My heart of flesh is tainted,

like spilled oil on fresh snow.

That's why I need You

to cleanse my blackened world of sin

and circumcise this heart of flesh

so my heart can be Your home.

*Create in me a pure heart, O God, and renew a
steadfast spirit within me.*

Psalm 51:10

Wandering

My heart wandered

    further and further

        from You,

yet, upon my return,

You washed the dust off my feet.

My spotless robe

When I see You, God,

in all Your glory,

with my heart exposed

and my every sin revealed,

my shame will condemn me.

I'll cower before Your throne,

knowing I'm worthy of wrath,

knowing I've fallen so short.

But here comes my Jesus:

my Mediator, my Passover Lamb.

He's carrying my spotless robe,

purified in His precious blood.

Now You look at me with love,

for Christ's righteousness covers me:

"Well done, my faithful child;

Come enjoy the heavenly feast."

Passover

I deserve every plague

to be thrown my way,

for I have hardened

my heart, just like Pharoah.

I deserve to be swallowed

in the raging Red Sea,

to be buried beneath

the justice of His wrath.

But like the Israelites in bondage,

Christ Jesus has broken my chains

and rescued me from oppressive reign.

When darkness fills the earth,

I am safe inside my home.

God's wrath passes over me,

for Christ's blood covers my soul.

Christ, our Passover Lamb, has been sacrificed.
1 Corinthians 5:7b

Fragments

Lord, sew together

this divided heart

with Your gentle hands.

Patch up the holes

that tore in my soul

when I ran away from You.

Take these scraps

and create a wardrobe

fit for Your kingdom.

For I am nothing more

than tainted fragments

without Your love.

But You see a quilt

in these fragments.

You see what I will become.

Co-heir

I'd be happy with

the lowliest place in heaven,

yet He elevates me to

a position I don't deserve.

He has promised me life

as a co-heir with Christ—

though of all sinners,

I am the worst.

*Here is a trustworthy saying that deserves full
acceptance: Christ Jesus came into the world to
save sinners—of whom I am the worst.*

1 Timothy 1:15

Surrender

This heart is a harbor for idols,

a shelter for sinful thoughts.

I hide my evil behind the fig leaves

as if You cannot see me.

But You know my heart completely.

You know each filthy rag I cling to,

yet You sew me better clothes.

You see that in this heart of darkness,

there's a desire for Your light.

You see that beneath my sinful state,

there's a child You'll make new.

You see me. You know me. You love me.

So I come out from behind the fig leaves

and show You my broken heart.

And You rejoice over me,

for I finally chose You.

I finally gave You my heart.

Humble ground

Humble hearts

are the root of repentance.

My contrite tears

water my soul.

And the Lord is more pleased

with my messy molehill

than a luxurious landscape

that is haughtily grown.

The Lord slips on His work gloves

and enters this place where dust abounds.

My lowly land is enough for Him,

for He builds gardens on humble ground.

*Humble yourselves, therefore, under God's
mighty hand, that he may lift you up in due time.*

1 Peter 5:6

Life

Lord, I owe You everything,

though I know this gift of life

is nothing I could ever earn.

You gave Your life so freely;

now all I want to do

is give You my life in return.

*If we live, we live for the Lord; and if we die, we
die for the Lord. So, whether we live or die, we
belong to the Lord.*

Romans 14:8

As I've loved you

Jesus tells me to show love to the hateful

and kindness to the ungrateful.

I imagine giving everything to someone

only to have them demand more.

And I have a hard time understanding

why I should turn to them my other cheek

when I'm the one who's sore.

I imagine walking the extra mile

only to hear them complain.

And I have a hard time understanding

why I should pray for my persecutors

when I'm the one in pain.

So Jesus looks me in the eyes and says,

"Love others as I've loved you."

And then I remember He's given me everything,

yet I've constantly demanded more.

I've slapped His cheek again and again,

yet it was my pain and suffering He bore.

He walked the extra mile,

the silent Lamb heading to be slain.

He prayed for those who murdered Him,

as His blood poured out like rain.

Jesus tells me to show love to the hateful

and kindness to the ungrateful

because that is exactly what He did for me.

I nailed Him to the cross, and He said,

"Father, forgive her."

And those same nails set me free.

Fragrant offerings

My humbled heart

echoes the praise

of a heavenly melody:

exalting His holy name,

thanking Him for His grace,

and marveling at the way

He can be both so perfectly.

My repentant heart

presents an offering

the Lord favors most:

the sweet fragrance

of a living sacrifice

that confesses their darkness

and chooses His light.

*For the LORD takes delight in his people; he
crowns the humble with victory.*

Psalm 149:4

My Gardener

I am a garden.

He is my Gardener.

He tills my soil tenderly.

He spreads the seeds.

He sends down soft rains

of living water.

He lights the sky with the Son.

He watches patiently as

His salvation sprouts its head.

He kindly cares for His garden

until the trees begin to bloom.

He glories in the sweet fruit,

trimming me gently to increase my yield.

He takes great pleasure in my growth,

longing for me to blossom more and more.

Sanctified

the process of becoming more like Jesus and less like the world through the work of the Holy Spirit; to increasingly desire to walk in holiness

May God himself, the God of peace, sanctify you through and through. May your whole spirit, soul, and body be kept blameless at the coming of our Lord Jesus Christ. The one who calls you is faithful, and he will do it.

1 Thessalonians 5:23-24

Living sacrifice

You're building me into a temple,

a spiritual house,

a holy place.

Your Spirit dwells within these walls,

cleansing me daily

with rivers of grace.

Your blood purifies my heart forever,

and I offer You daily

my first fruits of praise.

I present my body as a living sacrifice,

dying to myself

so I can live out Your ways.

Daily, I tear down the idols,

for You are worth more

than silver and gold.

And this is my true act of worship,

living for the One

who purchased my soul.

The cost

There's a cost to following Jesus,

but it's the greatest purchase you'll make,

for the sacrifice pales in comparison

to the abundant life that awaits.

Then Jesus said to his disciples, "Whoever wants to be my disciple must deny themselves and take up their cross and follow me."

Matthew 16:24

Undivided

To be a friend with the world

is to be an enemy with You.

Lord, my members are waging war;

I'm hard pressed between the two.

For I often seek after my own glory

and find satisfaction in this life,

though I know You deserve all glory

and only You can satisfy.

Lord, please give me a heart that's undivided,

for I'm still caught between the two.

I cannot bear to be double minded;

Lord, help me long for none but You.

I want to despise what You despise

and desire what You desire.

I want to see this life through Your eyes,

and in all I do, exalt You higher.

I want to be Your friend,

and leave this sinful world behind.

For when this temporary place meets its end,

I will be Your friend for life.

Spiritual warfare

Evil parades itself on the stages

of the celebrities we adore,

for the serpent's use of golden calves

is his greatest weapon of war.

And this is satan's evil scheme:

to desensitize us to the darkness

and all that is unclean.

But as I fill my mind with Christ,

He clothes me in His righteousness

and shows me His path of light.

And I follow after Him, even though it means

leaving much of this world behind.

For lucifer longs to lure me,

but I'd much rather cling to Christ.

*Our struggle is not against flesh and blood, but
against the rulers, against the authorities, against
the powers of this dark world and against the
spiritual forces of evil in the heavenly realms.*

Ephesians 6:12

More of Him

The devil works in advertising,

convincing us we need more to feed our flesh

and less and less of God,

persuading us to feast on folly

and squander all we have

to achieve a life of peace and comfort,

as if he could even offer us this.

Jesus works in our hearts,

convincing us we need more and more of Him

and less of this world that is wasting away,

persuading us to feast on His goodness

and share all we have with others

so they may know of what He offers:

an eternity of true peace and comfort.

Mission

My mind believed in You,

but my heart did not treasure You.

I walked with one foot in the world

and one foot in the pew.

Still, You walked beside me

and kindled a fire in my soul.

You made Your purposes my plan

and Your glory my goal.

Now my mission in this life

is to bring this world to Christ,

walking through the darkness

to display Your wondrous light.

Ally

In the battlefield of my mind,

my flesh is waging war

against His Spirit within me.

My body and my soul are not allies.

My soul thirsts for the goodness of God,

yet my body would stand in the line of fire

for a taste of what this world offers.

Daily, He reminds me

to carry my cross to Calvary.

And there, I see my Perfect Ally

securing victory.

United with my Ally in death,

I've risen to new life.

And with His strength,

I'm killing off my sinful ways

and fighting on His side.

*So I say, walk by the Spirit, and you will not gratify
the desires of the flesh. For the flesh desires what
is contrary to the Spirit, and the Spirit what is
contrary to the flesh.*

Galatians 5:16-17a

Paradox

He's blooming in me a life-giving tree,

bearing in me the sweet fruits produced

from His rivers of grace within.

Yet, He's also training up a mighty warrior,

arming me with valiant weapons of truth

to fight the daily battle of sin.

This is the paradox of becoming like Christ—

though gentle and kind,
equipped for the fight;

though crucified daily,
raised to new life.

New creation

I'm being transformed

from worldly to godly,

dying to the person I was

because You have made me someone new.

I'm being transformed

from self-seeking to serving,

letting go of what I once desired

because my greatest desire is You.

*Therefore, if anyone is in Christ, the new creation
has come: The old has gone, the new is here!*

2 Corinthians 5:17

True beauty

Earthly concerns are slipping away,

for I'm no longer coveting man's empty praise

or painting perfection onto my face.

I'm looking in the mirror less and less

and feeling less need to dress up my flesh,

for what You find beautiful is faithfulness.

Society's standards are too shallow for me,

for as I dive deeper into Your saving sea,

I see that true beauty is Jesus in me.

A temple among ruins

The world doesn't recognize me

as its own anymore,

for I am a temple among ruins

and a light among darkness.

The world preaches its way of life:

"Always put yourself first."

"Don't let others tell you how to live."

"Chase after your dreams."

But the Spirit has raised me to a new way of life:

"Always count others above yourself."

"Live your life to please the Lord."

"Chase after God's heart."

The world doesn't recognize me

as its own anymore,

and it shouldn't,

for I am not of this world.

They are not of the world, even as I am not of it.
John 17:16

Abdication

I am no longer

the lord of my life.

I am tearing down

the throne room I built

in my heart.

I am giving up

my fabricated reign as queen.

For I have been purchased

by the precious,

life-giving blood

of the King of Kings.

I'd rather bow down to His throne

than pretend to have my own.

Crucified with Christ

I'm crucifying worldliness

in a culture that preaches its power.

Society sells tips for success,

but I see its consumers drowning in

the never-ending debt

of remaining relevant.

I'm crucifying these desires

in a culture that idolizes self.

Society urges me to leave a mark,

but the only marks

worth bearing in this life

are the marks of following Christ.

*For we know that our old self was crucified with
him so that the body ruled by sin might be done
away with, that we should no longer be slaves to
sin.*

Romans 6:6

Transformed

"You've changed."

Yeah, I have.

What do you expect

from a ransomed slave?

After what my Redeemer did for me,

how could I ever stay the same?

King of my heart

This world extends an invitation

to drink the cup of demons,

a cup I was once familiar with.

The prince of peer pressure

labors to persuade me

that it's okay to take a sip.

But I'd rather taste the fruit of the Spirit,

for the Holy of Holies has become

the King of my heart.

Holiness is now my way of life,

and the way of this world cannot persuade me,

for my King has set me apart.

*No one can serve two masters. Either you will hate
the one and love the other, or you will be devoted
to the one and despise the other.*

Matthew 6:24a

Renamed

I've been renamed with

the most precious name of all: holy.

The Name Above All Names

chose to share His name with me.

He gifted me His Spirit,

to lead me in righteousness

and reflect just a glimmer

of the Light who lives in me.

When the world labels me and mocks me,

I'll gladly wear that crown of thorns.

For I've been renamed with

the greatest title of all:

ambassador of the Lord.

Clothed in Christ

In the wardrobe of my heart,

there are two different sets of clothes:

the filthy rags I wore in slavery

and the Spirit's righteous robe.

I have a choice to put on my old self

or the new man I'm called to be.

And Christ teaches me to daily choose

the clothes He has designed for me.

I'm undressing myself of ungodliness

and wearing tenderness, humility, and love.

I'm undressing myself of impurity

so I reflect Christ's kingdom above.

Put on the new self, created to be like God in true righteousness and holiness.

Ephesians 4:24

Reflection

The moon has no power

without the sun's light.

It cannot shine alone;

it reflects the sun at night.

In the same way, I long to be

a light for all to see:

gleaming through the darkness

though the light is not from me.

The moon is a reflection.

Its brilliance is not its own.

I long to be the same:

a pure reflection of the Son.

Like a child

To be sanctified is

to become like a child;

to be unshaken when storms surround me

because my gaze is locked on You;

to be overflowing with joy each day

because I see Your goodness everywhere;

to be humble in every step I take

because I know I'm dependent on You;

to be content with not knowing everything

because I trust the world is in Your care;

to be loving, gentle, lowly, and kind

because I imitate all I learn from You.

*Truly I tell you, unless you change and become
like little children, you will never enter the
kingdom of heaven.*

Matthew 18:3

Love in action

May I truly love as You did:
not just in my head,
but in my heart, hands, and feet.
Love is not meant to be hidden,
so may my faith be shown alive
by Your Spirit working in me.

May I truly love as You did:
humbly placing others first,
servant-minded with every breath.
Love is meant to be lived out,
so may my selfish wants be crucified
as I surrender to You in every step.

Living faith

If a tree planted by You must bear fruit,

then bear every sort of fruit in me.

Till the soil where sin still stands,

and in its place, plant righteous seeds.

If a genuine faith in You yields a harvest,

then, Lord, prune me through and through.

Clip me, trim me, shape me, grow me

so my fruit makes known my faith in You.

As the body without the spirit is dead, so faith without deeds is dead.

James 2:26

His name

This world tells me

to make a name for myself.

But the persuasion of power

and seduction of success

no longer has a pull on me.

For I'm not connected to those chains;

Jesus Christ has set me free.

This world tells me

to make a name for myself.

But I'm taking up my cross

and renouncing glory and fame.

For my only mission in this world

is to magnify His name.

(Un)cancel culture

When I am wronged,

may grudges never form in my heart.

When I am cursed,

may prayers of blessing fall from my lips.

When I am insulted,

may forgiveness flow from my soul.

When I am reviled as Jesus was,

may Jesus be seen in me.

But I tell you, love your enemies and pray for those who persecute you.

Matthew 5:44

Fulfillment

Fill the valleys in me with living water

that I may overflow Your life-giving love

into the valleys of those around me.

Bring low my mountains of pride

that I may humbly serve others

to show that Jesus lives through me.

Set straight any crooked way in me

that I may fix my feet upon Your path

and lead others through the narrow gate.

Level out the rocky soil in me

that Your Word may implant me deeply

so I can bear more fruit each day.

*Every valley shall be filled in, every mountain and
hill made low. The crooked roads shall become
straight, the rough ways smooth. And all people
will see God's salvation.*

Luke 3:5-6

Imago Dei

I'm being sanctified,

but I'm far from sinless.

Still, I'm on the narrow path:

the road of daily repentance.

For I no longer glory in my sins.

I've grown to hate them more and more.

And I long for the day that's coming:

when my Imago Dei is fully restored.

I'm running the race,

but I'm far from perfected.

And I long for the day that's coming:

when God's glory in me is resurrected.

Promise

God's will for you in Christ

is a promise, not a possibility.

He who rescued you has justified you.

He who justified you is sanctifying you.

He who is sanctifying you will glorify you.

Rather than pressure, you have peace.

Rather than striving, you have rest.

Rather than uncertainty, you have hope.

For He who began the work in you

will never leave you unfinished.

*He who began a good work in you will carry it on
to completion until the day of Christ Jesus.*

Philippians 1:6

The finish line

Sometimes, this life is heavy.

You're straining to carry your cross.
You're toiling to finish the race.
You're fighting the urge to break down.
But darling, you're not giving up.

And, sometimes, that's all God expects of us.

The truth is, you've never looked more like Christ
than in this very moment:
when you press on toward the Father
though your flesh is bleeding out.

Glorified

the transformation of our bodies when we are united with Jesus; to be brought to a perfect condition in body and spirit

Dear friends, now we are children of God, and what we will be has not yet been made known. But we know that when Christ appears, we shall be like him, for we shall see him as he is.

1 John 3:2

All the while

Oh, what a journey it's been:

growing in grace

and growing in Him.

What once was dead and depraved

has been made alive in Him.

Each day, I'm one step closer,

yet He has loved me all the same.

For all the while, I've been loved,

loved enough to save.

Oh, what a journey it's been:

from fallen to forgiven,

from guilty to justified.

All the while, I've been loved,

loved enough to glorify.

You were washed, you were sanctified, you were justified in the name of the Lord Jesus Christ and by the Spirit of our God.

1 Corinthians 6:11b

Fit for Eden

I look back on my days spent on the earth,

the days before I knew Him,

when I danced in delight of my sin.

And then I remember the day He rescued me

and began His work in my heart

so it would reflect His more and more.

Even after He befriended me,

I wandered away at times.

But like the Gracious Shepherd He is,

He brought me safely back to Him,

promising me that one day

I would never wander again.

Soon, I will finally live up to

the holy title He's given me.

He will restore in me

a body fit for Eden.

This earthly body

This earthly body is a temple of promise,

constructed with a foundation of hope,

bricks of grace, stones of love.

This earthly body holds a Spirit from heaven,

poured into my cement heart

to bring me life, to raise me up.

This earthly body is a temporary home,

but the Spirit inside is a down payment,

a guarantee of the inheritance to come.

*[The Spirit] is a deposit guaranteeing our
inheritance until the redemption of those who are
God's possession—to the praise of his glory.*

Ephesians 1:14

How sweet it will be

How sweet it will be

when His lips speak my name,

when He reads from the book of life.

How sweet it will be

when He welcomes me home,

when He shows me the way to the river of life.

How sweet it will be

when His eternal plan unfolds,

when He gives me a taste of the tree of life.

How sweet it will be

when my faith becomes sight,

when I finally see the true meaning of life.

Resurrected

True hope lives in the empty tomb.

If Christ died but never rose,

we'd have nothing to hold on to

but a liar who returned to the dust.

Every promise he made

would have been buried with him,

and all we would have to look forward to

is the day we join him in the ground.

But Christ walked out of the grave.

He lives and reigns eternally

both in heaven and our hearts.

Every promise He made

is being resurrected in us.

True hope dwells within my soul—

for I know my tomb will be empty too.

If only for this life we have hope in Christ, we are of all people most to be pitied.

1 Corinthians 15:19

My version of heaven

What do you think heaven will be like?

I picture all of God's children

crowded around His throne.

We're asking Him questions,

and He's telling us stories,

unveiling mysteries our earthly bodies

always longed to know.

I picture us sitting on His lap,

soaking in every single word.

It's like we're children again,

consumed with awe and wonder,

with no dream of leaving home.

Glorious day

Oh, how we long for that glorious day

when our sanctification meets its end.

Oh, how we imagine the wondrous reunion

with our undying bodies, free of sin.

Oh, how we groan for the Almighty's embrace,

approaching His throne of grace with no fear.

Oh, how we hold on to His promises

as this glorious day draws near.

*We ourselves, who have the first fruits of the
Spirit, groan inwardly as we wait eagerly for our
adoption to sonship, the redemption of our
bodies.*

Romans 8:23

Perfection

This flesh has wrestled with God often.

These hands have not served Him fully.

This heart has not loved Him wholly.

This mind has not trusted Him perfectly.

But the day is coming when

this broken body will be raised in power,

and my hands, my heart, and my mind

will fully, wholly, and perfectly worship Him.

This earthly mind that is being renewed

will be instantly transformed,

and this wrestle between my flesh and my spirit

will finally come to an end.

The thief and his deceit will be destroyed,

and my relationship with God will never be

riddled with doubt or lacking joy again.

I'll enter His rest and hang up my shield,

and the fruit He's been growing in me

will finally reach a perfect yield.

Immanuel

Our God has always been

a God of presence:

God with us in the garden,

God with us in the manger,

God with us in our hearts.

And now, the day is coming

when the meaning of Immanuel

will be illuminated forevermore:

His presence tangibly felt,

His love fully realized,

His Eden completely restored.

*And I heard a loud voice from the throne saying,
"Look! God's dwelling place is now among the
people, and he will dwell with them. They will be
his people, and God himself will be with them and
be their God."*

Revelation 21:3

Face to face

Lord, when we see You face to face,

every knee will bow before Your holiness.

You will cleanse Your promised land

of every tongue who rejected You,

and these souls will see

Your righteous wrath face to face.

You will welcome into Your kingdom

every heart who longed for You,

and these souls will see

Your exponential grace face to face.

Lord, when we see You face to face,

we will truly understand

how undeserved Your favor is.

Yet You freely give it to Your children.

You graciously welcome us in.

Saturated

Those who thirsted for You

and Your righteousness

will be saturated in it.

You will immerse them

in eternal waters,

forever washing clean

their every imperfection.

You will heal their human condition

by stilling anxious minds,

refreshing tired souls,

and renewing feeble hearts.

Everyone who followed You,

though they often fell short,

will never fall again.

But our citizenship is in heaven. And we eagerly await a Savior from there, the Lord Jesus Christ, who ... will transform our lowly bodies so that they will be like his glorious body.

Philippians 3:20-21

Shabbat

In the days of old,

God blessed man with a physical rest,

harkening back to

His work of creation

and pointing forward to

His work of redemption.

In the days of Christ,

God blessed man with a spiritual rest,

harkening back to

His promise of freedom

and pointing forward to

His promise of restoration.

In the days to come,

God will bless man with a final rest,

a true Shabbat that will endure for all time.

Like in the days of old,

God and man will rest together

in a glorious and untainted world:

body, soul, and mind in perfect Shabbat.

*There remains, then, a Sabbath-rest for the people
of God; for anyone who enters God's rest also
rests from their works, just as God did from his.*

Hebrews 4:9-10

The greatest gift

The Giver of All Good

has blessed us with many gifts:

with laughter and love,

with sunsets and songbirds,

with food to satisfy our stomachs,

breath to fill our lungs,

and His Spirit to guide our hearts.

But when we enter the immense glory

of His perfect kingdom,

we shall see that He has saved

the greatest gift for last:

an eternity with Him.

I have seen you in the sanctuary and beheld your power and your glory. Because your love is better than life, my lips will glorify you.

Psalm 63:2-3

Treasure

Entering His sanctuary,

I'm overwhelmed by the weight of glory.

More breathtaking than a thousand sunrises,

more powerful than ten thousand stormy waves,

and yet more peaceful

than any calm I've known.

Entering His pearly gates,

I'm awestruck by the riches of His love.

More splendid than a thousand bars of gold,

more glorious than ten thousand precious stones,

and now, I'm humbled

that He has called me His own.

Communion

Everything I thought

would fill me

fell so short.

My cup is overflowing

as I enter Your courts above.

Everything I thought

would bring me joy

did not compare.

My joy is made complete

in the communion of Your love.

*You make known to me the path of life; you will
fill me with joy in your presence, with eternal
pleasures at your right hand.*

Psalm 16:11

Throne room

I enter Your most holy place

where wickedness is instantly struck down.

I bow before Your righteous throne,

and I'm more alive than ever.

For I've been clothed in a holiness

worthy of entering Your presence:

not a holiness of my own

but of Christ's blood washing over me.

I join in with the saints and angels,

singing holy, holy

for this wretched, wretched sinner

has a place before Your throne.

Multiplied

His children from every land

proclaiming His praises

in a heavenly tongue:

different cultures knit together

in the united language of His love.

Every brother and sister

from every tribe throughout all time:

thousands of years in the making,

God's love story fulfilled,

the garden's glory multiplied.

*After this I looked, and there before me was a
great multitude that no one could count, from
every nation, tribe, people and language, standing
before the throne and before the Lamb.*

Revelation 7:9a

Adoption day

He welcomes His children home:

opening His arms to the fatherless,

binding the wounds of the abused,

cherishing the neglected,

and overwhelming the hearts of those

who were loved well on the earth.

The fatherless enjoy a warm embrace

for the first time.

The abused experience the gentle touch

they've longed to feel.

The neglected hear the affectionate words

of a proud Father.

Those loved well on the earth realize

they encountered only a taste.

For when He welcomes His children home,

they discover a love far greater

than any love they've ever known.

Wedding banquet

He welcomes me home

to my promised inheritance.

He smiles as my soul

worships Him fully.

He washes me clean

as I enter His banquet.

He clothes me

in everlasting robes.

He seats me at His table

in a place of honor.

He serves me a heavenly feast,

and I worship Him all the more.

For even in His glorious kingdom,

my Master's heart delights to serve.

It will be good for those servants whose master finds them watching when he comes. Truly I tell you, he will dress himself to serve, will have them recline at the table and will come and wait on them.

Luke 12:37

Anointed

My heart was polluted with pride

until the day You brought me low.

You poured oil over me

and anointed my weary soul.

From polluted to anointed,

from Hell bound to Heaven blessed:

You took away my spoiled clothes

and dressed me in Heaven's best.

Victorious

I'm hanging up the armor of God:

the belt of truth,

for deception has been slain;

the breastplate of righteousness,

for all that is unrighteous has been destroyed;

the gospel on my feet,

for the good news to share is known by all;

the shield of faith,

for the unseen is now before my eyes;

the helmet of salvation,

for I am safe from danger

with my Refuge forever;

the sword of the Spirit,

for the Word has reigned victorious

over every spiritual war.

I'm hanging up the armor of God,

for I'm forever loved in His forever land

where sin and death are no more.

It's everything I've ever hoped for.

Heavenly feast

Feasting on the Bread of Life,

I hunger for nothing more.

Cleansed in His living water,

my parched soul has been restored.

I'm reclining at the table

with the Lamb who died for me.

The Last Supper, never-ending.

My dirty feet, forever clean.

*Whoever drinks the water I give them will never
thirst. Indeed, the water I give them will become
in them a spring of water welling up to eternal life.*

John 4:14

Untainted

One day,

you will look into the eyes of Jesus Christ and

every worldly worry that kept you up at night

will finally fall from your fingertips.

Your burdens will be lifted in an instant.

Your anxieties will be calmed.

In His eyes, you'll see

justice that you've never seen before.

In His arms, you'll find

the peace you couldn't feel on this earth.

In His smile, you'll feel

the welcoming grace you've longed to know.

And on that day,

you will look into the eyes of Jesus Christ and

you will be transformed in an instant.

Your sinful flesh will burn in His hands

along with the rest of this weeping world.

Your ceaseless striving,

your harrowing questions,

the sins that kept knocking at your door,

they will all vanish like vapor.

And on that day,

when you look into the eyes of Jesus Christ,

you will finally understand

the likeness of God.

Your body of flesh will be buried in the past.

You will look into Christ's living river

and see the redemption plan

meet its end in the beginning:

where the God of the universe

walks alongside His love

in a garden untainted by sin.

Now that you have been set free from sin and have become slaves of God, the benefit you reap leads to holiness, and the result is eternal life.

Romans 6:22